The Confessions

Alexander Zeldin

methuen | drama

LONDON • NEW YORK • OXFORD • NEW DELHI • SYDNEY

METHUEN DRAMA
Bloomsbury Publishing Plc
50 Bedford Square, London, WC1B 3DP, UK
1385 Broadway, New York, NY 10018, USA
29 Earlsfort Terrace, Dublin 2, Ireland

BLOOMSBURY, METHUEN DRAMA and the Methuen
Drama logo are trademarks of Bloomsbury Publishing Plc

First published in Great Britain 2023

Cover design by Rebecca Heselton

Cover image: *Pierrot* (formerly known as Gilles) by
Jean Antonie Watteau, c. 1718–19, oil on canvas, 184.5 x 149 cm
© Tuul and Bruno Morandi / Alamy Stock Photo

A catalogue record for this book is available from the British Library.

A catalog record for this book is available from the Library of Congress.

ISBN: PB: 978-1-3504-5672-3
ePDF: 978-1-3504-5673-0
eBook: 978-1-3504-5674-7

Series: Modern Plays

Typeset by Mark Heslington Ltd, Scarborough, North Yorkshire

To find out more about our authors and books visit
www.bloomsbury.com and sign up for our newsletters.

The Confessions was originally produced by A Zeldin Company/Compagnie A Zeldin and had its world premiere at the Volkstheater as part of Vienna Festwochen, on 14 June 2023 with the following cast and creative team:

Cast

Graham/Terry/Librarian	Joe Bannister
Older Alice	Amelda Brown
Eldon/Joss	Jerry Killick
Pat/Leander	Lilit Lesser
Bob/Freddy/Jacob	Brian Lipson
Alice	Eryn Jean Norvill
Peg/Viv/Eva	Pamela Rabe
Susie	Gabrielle Scawthorn
Rossy/Leigh/Student/Robbie	Yasser Zadeh

Creatives

Director Alexander Zeldin
Set and Costume Designer Marg Horwell
Choreographer and Movement Director Imogen Knight
Lighting Designer Paule Constable
Composer Yannis Philippakis
Sound Designer Josh Anio Grigg
Casting Director Jacob Sparrow
Australian Casting Serena Hill
Associate Director Joanna Pidcock
Dramaturgs Faye Merralls, Sasha Milavic Davies
Voice Director Cathleen MacCarron
Dialect Coaches Louise Jones, Jenny Kent

Co-commissioned by the National Theatre; RISING Melbourne; Les Théâtres de la Ville de Luxembourg.

Co-produced by Wiener Festwochen; Comédie de Genève; Odéon-Théâtre de l'Europe; Centro Cultural de Belém; Théâtre de Liège; Festival d'Avignon; Festival d'Automne à Paris; Athens Epidaurus Festival; Piccolo Teatro di Milano –

Teatro d'Europa; Adelaide Festival; Centre Dramatique National de Normandie-Rouen.

The original production was sponsored by Nancy and Michael Timmers, Cas Donald, David Schwimmer, Elisabeth de Kergorlay, Mazdak Rassi and Zanna Roberts Rassi, Andrew and Raquel Segal, Victoria Reese and Greg Kennedy, Studio Indigo Architects & Interior Designers.

The Confessions subsequently ran from 19 October to 4 November 2023 at the Lyttelton Theatre, National Theatre (producer: Adowa-Alexsis Mintah).

The Confessions

A note on the text

A '.' indicates a thought that doesn't become a word.

A '/' indicates an interruption, where the following line of dialogue begins to be spoken.

Prologue

A large red curtain is drawn across the stage. At the moment of the performance.

Older Alice, *80, who is sitting in the audience, goes up on stage.*

When she is there she waits a time for the audience to quieten down. She speaks as if speaking to someone in the audience directly.

Older Alice   When I was a little girl, there were not many men around, they were all in the war. The first time I met a man, I was convinced he was deceiving me. I was terrified of him, sure that he was trying to trick me.

I remember, I am four or five years old, in the front room of my parents' house in Kiama, New South Wales. At that time, in Kiama, the children were very free, roaming across the hills unsupervised. It was a different time.

I am sitting on the floor, talking to my doll.

A man in a uniform walks in in silence. He stands there gazing at me for quite a long time. I thought my mother would follow but she wasn't there.

He comes up, squats over me. Looks down.

She smiles.

'I AM YOUR DADDY!' he says.

'You are not my daddy! That,' I said, pointing to a picture on the wall, 'is my daddy.'

She points to the audience, the fourth wall, as if the paintings are on the wall.

He is upset. 'That is a picture of me, I painted it!'

You're not him, I said.

'Well, that's because it's a painting and I'm a person, and we're not the same.'

He said to me.

I always thought that painting *was* my father. And now I'd lost him. I get confused you see. I'm not in on the joke but watching it from outside. I think my parents knew I wasn't very clever, bless them.

A decent-length pause. She might think about going back to the audience.

See. I'm not interesting. I'm an old lady, what's so interesting about me . . . I can't say anything of interest to you . . .

Short pause. Thinking to herself. Almost talking to herself, she now just says what comes into her head.

My parents protected me too much. Maybe because I was an only child. I was sent away at fifteen to a boarding school they couldn't afford, because they were worried the local surfers would impregnate me.

Laughs.

She now turns and draws the curtains across the stage, revealing another stage behind it, a kind of school hall from the 1950s, with a small theatre at the back of it, with a microphone on it. It is set as if for an event. She goes up to the smaller stage and draws the curtains. A time. As soon as she's gone through, **Younger Alice** (*hereafter referred to as* **Alice**) *comes through the curtain.*

Act One

One

1959

Alice *comes through the curtain, looks out into the hall, taps on the microphone and attempts to speak, but doesn't.*

Alice

Pat *and* **Susie** *enter. All of the school girls are dressed in ball dresses.*

Pat   Shh, Alice!

Alice   S/orry!

They wander to the front of the stage. Silence. A feeling of them having broken into the room.

Susie   So this is where we'll dance and / lalala

Alice   Oh yes.

Pat   What if we are here when the cadets come in?

Susie   Well then, we'll be the first ones that they see.

Pause, they stand as if they are mannequins in a window display. For quite a long time, maybe 20 seconds.

Pat   I need to pee.

Susie   Again?

Pat *stays.*

Alice   Susie! I love your dress.

Susie   It's undressable.

She shows how easy it is to get out of it, it's funny.

In case.

Alice   Oh!

Susie   It's European.

So, this is it, the dance.

Alice   Yes! The *end* of it all.

Susie *eyes* **Pat** *up. They hear another noise. Silence, looking out for Godot.*

Pat   Phew, no-one.

Susie   What are *you* wearing?

Patricia*'s dress is too short for her and unfashionable.*

Pat   My dress.

Susie   What is that?

Pat   It's my dress, my mother's.

Susie   What can a girl do to make someone like her / when she . . .

Pat   It's my only dress, don't be so unkind /

Susie   Who's going to dance with you in that?

Susie *sings very very briefly into the microphone.*

Alice/Pat   Shh . . .

Silence, they wander around.

Susie   The end of school at LAST.

Alice   Gosh, well, I'm so excited to go to uni but /

Susie   Golly Burns, what a thrill.

Alice   Yes. I'm interested in having my own ideas you know /

Pat   Gosh you're lucky. I'm done with learning.

Alice   My parents have saved up.

Pat   Oh! But you are in the bottom set / in nearly all subjects.

Alice   Not art.

Susie   You can be so cruel Pat.

I'm just getting out of here and going to Europe, I'm not marrying any of these /

Noise.

Alice   What is that?

Pat   They are coming . . .

Susie   Hurrah!

Pat   Hide, they can't see us here.

Susie   Ah no /

Pat   Hide!

They could find a way of looking out of the room, to build this moment longer. They scatter. **Alice** *and* **Susie** *through the curtain.*

Enter **Graham** *and* **Rossy**, *two Naval Cadets in full uniform.*

Giggles from behind the curtain.

Graham *approaches the curtain.*

Rossy   Graham.

Graham *goes closer to the curtain.*

Graham   Come on!

Rossy   . . .

They jump up and slide in behind the curtain. There are shrieks and noises and they all talk at once. It is quite important that we don't make out the words. It can be ad libbed, as it isn't important that it is heard exactly.

Susie   *Ah!!! You're not meant to be / here ah!!!*

Graham   *Good evening /*

Pat   *Patricia!*

Etc.

Then there is a silence.

Two

A year or so later.

The curtains on the small school theatre stage open to reveal a perfectly realised kitchen. Alice and her parents **Bob** *(50-ish) and* **Peg** *(forties) are there at a round table. There is a suitcase –* **Alice** *has just returned from university. There can be a bit of business, a sense of not being able to speak.*

Peg   I made *a lot* of juice.

Bob   It's very good though, the juice, have some it/'s

Pause while she drinks.

Alice   Wow it's really good. It's really good Mum.

Another pause – a look between the parents. At least 8 seconds. Full of false starts.

Peg   We were expecting you yesterday, / see.

Alice   So sorry.

Peg   I'll get you more.

Alice   I didn't pass, I'm sorry. I did my best but I couldn't, you know it was. I failed first year and, well, I'm out.

Bob   Oh.

Darling I'm sorry, well that's / ok.

Alice   I'll pay you back the money, I mean the spending money you gave me Dad / actually and I'm gonna try.

Peg   Don't think about that. You gave it a go. Forget it now.

Peg *gives her a hug, it is very quick.*

Alice (*jovial for her mother*)   Well . . . I did my best /

Peg   I blame the school, we paid so much /

Bob   Yeh, you just gotta try your best, and you, well, you try one thing and then you try another and in the end you'll find your way.

Short pause.

The world's your / oyster.

Peg   I'll get the rest.

Peg *goes off – saying under her breath that she's going to wash her hands.*

Bob   Did your friend Susie?

Alice   Well she's gallivanting around Europe having all sorts of love affairs, or something. Working in artistic / circles.

Bob   There are some magical paintings in Europe. Watteau, you know, my favourite. Sad bugger.

Alice   It's so hard to know what to do, Dad. I don't know what to do.

Bob   You stay 'true unto thyself and thou, thou thou can do no harm', like the wise Polonius said in William Shakespeare.

Alice   I just got so confused.

I was mute in the tutorials, Dad, I couldn't speak I was so shy.

Enter **Peg**.

Bob   Well darling, you can go back.

Peg *laughs briefly.*

Peg   We just want to do

What's right for you.

Alice   Mum I'm trying to talk to Dad? What do yo/u

Peg   But what, you know, the teaching scholarship you have to /

Older Alice *crosses the stage. No-one reacts to her.*

Alice   I'm not a primary teacher / Mum I want to . . .

Peg   What about your cousin Christine Jan Pat /

Alice   There are other girls who aren't just doing the jobs everyone says.

Peg   We sent you to a good school, a proper environment.

Alice   I just wanted to go to uni . . . Dad?

Bob   Sorry I had something I want to . . .

Alice   Yes Dad, what should I do?

Bob   Well . . . I . . . think your mother has some thoughts / I'll just . . .

He goes out.

Peg   You should talk to Gray now, darling /

Alice   Why did Dad stop painting?

Peg   Well he couldn't make a living on it.

Alice   But /

Perhaps a little defensive:

Peg   We kept a way of looking at things . . . a way of looking, seeing the garden, the flower arrangements.

Laughs.

I never went gallivanting!

Alice *looks out into the audience, allowing us to imagine paintings that she is seeing there.* **Older Alice** *is standing in the stalls looking at her.*

Alice   The paintings though /

Peg   You know, darling, you shouldn't keep Graham waiting on an answer forever.

Alice   I'm not, no no, I'm not keeping him waiting.

I told him, it'd be next year, you know next year at the earliest . . .

I wanted to finish uni, you / know.

Peg   Well that's over now. You gave it a go but don't get above yourself. You need to secure your future.

Graham will do that for you.

Alice   Yes . . . Mum?

Peg   You should accept him. You've had your experiments, now you'd be safe. The world is full of hard surfaces.

Alice   Mum. I'm safe.

Peg *has a little laugh.*

Alice   Gray said his family are / in Shoalhaven this weekend.

Peg   Yes, I said that he should pop by!

Alice   Mum?

Peg   I telegrammed him for his birthday / and mentioned you'd be here.

Alice   You didn't tell me!

Enter **Bob**.

Peg   It'd be terrific to see him.

Bob   I wanted to talk about the university! /

Peg   You don't need to go back you know, you're charming the way you are.

Alice   Yes, I think I'll stop. What was I thinking.

Peg   You've made the right choice dear.

Bob   What have you two /

Alice   But Dad maybe I can find a way to do some things in the evenings, you know there are several options for evening classes.

Bob   Yes.

Bob *wants to say something*.

Alice   Well yes, I mean I don't think I was cut out for university really, so.

Laughs.

I'm just not very / clever!

Bob   No don't (*doorbell rings*) you ever say / that Alice . . .

Peg   Oh that must be Gray, I'll . . .

Alice *dashes off to answer the door before* **Peg**.

Alice   Right, yes.

Alice *is gone. Silence.*

Peg   Do you think I should make some more /

Enter **Alice** *and* **Graham**.

Alice   Oh what a thrill to see you!

Gosh!

Peg   Oh how wonderful to see you!

Bob   Graham.

Beat.

Graham   Dear Mr and Mrs Burns, oh it is such a pleasure, I do hope / I'm not intruding.

Peg   No!

Graham   The Betlams are weekending / in Shoalhaven.

Alice   In Shoalhaven.

Peg   And it was your birthday.

Graham   Ah no / I, yes, thank you for the telegram.

Bob   Happy / birthday.

Graham   Thank you / my somewhat quiet and pensive nature makes me steer away from any excessive celebrations though!

I remember Alice / asking me that evening if I felt any different but . . . I don't think so. Most people were surprised to think I was only 21!

Peg   Yes / oh / indeed, gee! Well you look . . .

Please sit down!

Graham   After you.

Beat, he looks out, and then they all do, to where the pictures are imagined to be.

What lovely pictures.

Alice   They're Dad's.

Bob   Oh.

Beat.

Alice   Oh! Do you want some orange juice?

Peg   I'll have to make some more. Let's pick some oranges, give me a hand Bob.

Graham and **Alice** *are left alone.*

Alice   Thank you for being so nice to them / they like you.

Graham   Golly no, goodness, they're such decent people.

Alice   Oh, and Dad's pictures.

Graham   Well they're so charming.

As the curtains close, **Older Alice** *comes up on stage and speaks to the audience as music plays.*

Older Alice   The sea was loud, bashing up against the cliff, it was loud the whole time

It was nearly at the top of the headland, and our house jutting over the cliff side.

The music swells again, and then, as soon as she begins speaking, it dips.

She walks along the curtains, towards the side of the stage, as if searching.

There was a table and then, well I remember the main room.

She's forgotten.

Three

Six and a bit years later.

1969

The room of **Alice** *and* **Graham**'s *house near the Naval Barracks outside Sydney.* **Alice** *and* **Graham** *are having a dinner party. It is the day before* **Graham** *is going to sea. There is a dining table with several chairs and behind it a kind of kitchen area.*

Graham, **Pat** (*who has since joined the Navy*) *and their neighbours* **Viv** *and* **Eldon** (*forties*) *are there.*

Alice *is sat in a more passive position, centre.* **Alice** *is staring out.*

Viv   The bulls, the bulls, we're mad about the bulls, Pat you saw them on the / slides.

Graham *gets up to get a beer and looks at* **Alice**.

Graham   Beer mate /

Eldon   Always.

Viv   Everything is so much more vivid in Europe, you know, the people, the animals, the colours of the buildings . . . of the landscape . . . / of the . . .

Eldon   That's a very Spanish-looking colour, Alice.

Alice   Oh this!

Beat.

Viv   Well it looks really lovely!

Short beat.

Alice   Thank you.

Graham   Alice is always spending so much / on clothes and . . .

A sudden flurry of activity and movement, around the task of hosting the dinner. **Graham** *is bringing two beers over.*

Eldon   Flamenco! That's it. Yeh. The gypsy that was in the /

Pat   Graham do you need / any

Alice   It's ok! But sorry I . . .

Beat. A short silence. **Pat** *serves* **Alice**.

Pat   Punch? Wine?

Alice   Punch, yes!

Eldon   Yeh it was amazing . . . really amazing /

Enter **Leigh** *(twenties) with books, the door is just open. He looks a little different to the other guests. Less formal.*

There is a beat of surprise.

Leigh   Sorry, I, it was open.

Graham   Who are you?

Alice   Hello!

A beat.

Leigh   Sorry, hi I'm / Leigh, don't mean to intrude . . .

Alice *goes to him.*

Alice   My friend Leigh!

Graham   Right.

Viv   Hi.

Eldon   Hello.

Beat.

Leigh   – I was just returning these . . .

He puts the books on the table. Short beat, people aren't sure how to behave.

Wow, your house /

Viv   Fantastic spot.

Alice   Oh yes, the waves get / loud.

Graham   'Right by the cliffside' they said, the agent /

Eldon   You could just fall off.

They look offstage.

Leigh   Oh yes, it's quite a drop.

He walks to the edge of the room, the stage, where the cliff is and the drop.

Eldon   Leigh I was just saying.

Leigh   Gosh /

Eldon   Yeh we saw this incredible performance in Cadiz, I've got a recording of the artist!

Viv   The bulls, the bulls.

Graham   I know, you said.

Eldon   It was in this bar by the sea and there was a dancer, a gypo, who looked just like you Alice.

Viv   We've got the slides! You missed the slides!

Leigh   Oh wow, slides.

Eldon   All you can ask of me in life is to go back to Cadiz, that's it. All I'm good for.

A beat. A short laugh from **Eldon***, who laughs at himself.*

Graham   Where is Pat (*he goes to look for her*), she's just gone out to the porch maybe /

Viv *has moved seats away from* **Eldon** *towards* **Leigh***.*

Viv   Hi I'm Viv, this is Eldon.

As **Graham***'s following* **Pat** *out:*

Leigh   I'll / get going. I was just returning . . .

Graham   Oh well, nice to meet you.

Leigh   Yeh. You too mate.

Graham *goes upstage, and exits the kitchen.* **Leigh** *goes as if to leave.*

Alice   NO! NO!

Gray, Gray!

Re-enter **Graham***.*

Alice   Leigh knows Susie.

Leigh   Susie Miller.

Alice   You know my friend Susie. She's the / one.

Graham   Right, yes, sorry.

Alice   Well she's been working in London with all the . . . the artists of the place and period.

She sounds wrong, knows it.

Viv   Do have some taramasalata?

Eldon   You missed the slides mate.

Leigh   Oh yeh? No I just / popped over for the books. / I meant to get here earlier but there was . . .

Pat   Yeh. There's people. Everywhere and . . .

Leigh   So I was stopped by the cars down the bottom because of that guy.

Graham   There's a security situation there, yes.

Leigh   Yeh I was surprised your door /

Graham   Well, no Alice, I mean you should have closed it! Sorry.

Alice   I've heard,

There's been. Sit, Leigh!

Leigh   Oh! Just for a minute.

Leigh *sitting should be something of an event. People have to move to give him space.*

Alice   Well this chap, he threw his wife off a cliff.

Pat   What's his name?

Gluck!! That's his name, he's a foreigner. Maybe he's a Nazi / refugee from the Second World War.

Leigh   Most of the refugees were Jews I think, but yeh!

Beat.

Alice   Well he just pushed her off.

Leigh   I think he did worse than that, he cut her up and then put her in his car, and he wrapped her up I think and he then /

Viv   That's gruesome, /

Alice   He drove to the cliff up the road and threw her off but the body, well, the body parts washed up on shore.

Pat   What did she do?

Leigh   She didn't do anything.

Graham   Well!

Leigh   He's just a violent nut.

Short beat.

Eldon   It's a violent world.

Viv   Who wants some more of this? If you'd like more?

Short beat.

Alice   Sorry /

Pat   Stupid girl – what did she do to get herself pushed off a cliff?

Graham   Alice, you're going to ruin everyone's appetite!

Alice   Yes! Oh! I'm sorry it is a creepy subject. Oh? Pat?

Pat   Oh what's your / books?

Alice   Leigh borrowed them.

Leigh   Yeh, some fascinating stuff there, have you / read.

Graham   Alice used to read so much when I met her, all these foreign authors.

What, Simone? Sorry she's the writer / I remember now.

Eldon   Simone, sounds sexy.

Graham   Not quite mate, it was feminist ideas.

Eldon   Was that her name?

Leigh   Simone de Beauvoir.

She's French . . . Paris?

Alice *loves this.*

Eldon   You know in Europe there are so many radical ideas and powerful sexy women.

Let me go and get that record from next door.

Viv   Discos muy bonitos!

Exit **Eldon**.

Short beat.

Leigh   'My life would be a beautiful story that would become true, bit by bit, as I told it to myself.' She said that, I find that / fascinating.

Pat   Golly!

Leigh *gets up to leave during the next line. Something about how* **Pat** *says the previous line should make him feel unwelcome.*

Alice   Shall we get ready for dessert. I mean! Ha! Leigh stay!

Leigh   I'm just heading /

Pat   Oh you're off!

Viv (*about the dessert*)   I'll do it!!

I brought it, it's um, well, trifle, but I've sort of done it my own kind of way, with heaps of alcohol.

Graham   I'll get a couple of beers /

Graham *goes to the kitchen.*

Leigh   I was just / going to head out I don't want to intrude or . . .

Alice   No no!

Leigh knows Susie!

Graham   The Hippy? you said.

Alice   Ha!

How is she? Susie.

Leigh   Oh great. Yeh she said to call her.

Alice   I MUST! I've been so busy.

Leigh   Yeh she's so good, like, she's back in Sydney and she's . . .

Graham   Oh?

Leigh   Yeh.

She's back and you know she's fucking Eva Mannings? I told you right? Yeh everyone was like, out of the blue! But / yeh turns out she's a fucking raging lesbian.

He laughs.

Alice   The poet.

Leigh   Yeh! It's really amazing and raw yeh. When I first met her she'd just got back from Italy, she was involved in some kind of peasant theatre thing or living in one of these communal social centres like they have there, I heard.

Graham   Did you want a beer?

Leigh   Yeh no I'm good on the punch thanks.

Viv   Strewth.

Beat.

Pat   Graham . . .

Leigh   Sorry should I not . . . have mentioned that.

Alice   No Graham and Viv? Viv?

They're right on yeh.

Graham   Yeh no.

He steps out. **Alice** *and* **Leigh** *are left more alone at the dinner table.* **Pat** *and* **Viv** *are in the kitchen area.*

Leigh   Yeh well. You should see her. Her uncle has given her a place, I mean you know her rich uncle, well they're all rich I think but yeh this one he's letting have this shop front in Redfern before it gets demolished, he's just giving it to her.

Alice   She's lucky.

She laughs.

Leigh   You should go down and see her!

Re-enter **Graham**.

Graham   So you two /

Leigh   I give Alice a lift to evening class. Yeh, the centre / for adult education?

Alice   Oh it's amazing, you know I told you Graham! The classes, /

Graham   Do you, ok.

Leigh   And you are in the war / army.

Graham   Navy.

Eldon *enters.*

Eldon   Tengo El Disco /

Alice   Yes, it's . . .

The following should go on simultaneously, conversations in the kitchen and the dinner table.

Viv   Muy bien.

Pat   Oh wow, Spain.

Graham   It's nice to meet a friend of Alice's.

Eldon   Did you, drive, do you drive? Leigh?

Alice   I'm just going to get the rest. (*Clearing the table.*)

Leigh   Yes, I drive.

Eldon   Good. And where's your missus, mate?

Leigh   Oh. I'm not married.

But I drive yeh.

Eldon   Ford / is it?

Pat   I've never been to Europe.

Graham   Yes, we got a Ford.

Viv   Yes. No you must.

Graham   No.

Well I'm no great mechanic.

Eldon   You can say that again neighbour.

Pat   I've never been off the ship.

Eldon   She's a good motor but you know . . .

Graham   No right I LOVE frankly, an American car / is . . .

Eldon   Right.

Graham   Well. I was just saying we got a Ford because we don't need so much servicing.

Pat   It's hot isn't it /

Alice *is cleaning up, doing dishes, clearing the table in general.*

Pat *is looking at the books again.*

Alice   Summer is!

Pat   Oh!

Alice   That's DH Lawrence you've got there?

Leigh   I dig Lawrence.

Graham   Right.

Leigh   Yeh I read him when I was first at uni and yeh I was asking myself all sorts of questions, you know what I mean.

Graham   Alice keeps saying she's going back to study!

Viv   What for /

Alice (*removing all the books – trying to steer the conversation away from the books now*)   Well it's an idea, I have, that . . . I was at uni.

Graham   But she couldn't / I mean.

Alice   Graham.

Graham (*to* **Leigh**)   She well, she failed the first year, but that's ok because you became a teacher and went to / teach the kiddies.

Leigh   Really, you never mentioned that?

Alice (*to* **Leigh**)   Yes, I BECAME a teacher because the year I failed I didn't manage the uni course, I mean to get a full BA, but it's nearly the same as a BA, you know teaching primary and well secondary.

Pat   I haven't got an intellectual bone in my body, HAHAHA!

Leigh   No I'm sure that's not true.

Graham   No that's a pretty accurate description of Pat there Leigh.

All Alice wants to do is study but with me away so much /

Leigh   In Vietnam?

Slight pause, nothing to say.

Graham   That's right, HMAS *Sydney* / we're sailing tomorrow.

Pat   Early doors /

Graham   Four months on board.

Alice   Yes, it's so nice to have you all here to send them off!

Eldon   Long time at sea without the Mrs I reckon. I see them in port.

With a few prozzies up and / coming over the gangway.

Alice   I think it's only the men that are up and cumming in that configuration.

A beat, it hasn't gone down well. Only **Leigh** *laughs.*

Alice   That trifle looks awfully good.

Leigh   No.

What do you do?

Beat.

Pat   No, I think I wasn't clear. I'm in the Royal Australian Navy, with Graham.

Alice   And Pat and I were at school together . . . with Susie!

Pat   But I've not seen anything. Or been anywhere, off the ship I mean.

Long pause, they eat, sound of the spoons clanging.

Viv   Well I suppose you've got to keep the communists out so the war goes on.

Pat   That's the thing, you see, well I reckon.

I reckon that if one pack, it's like a pack of cards really there Val, /

Viv   Viv, my name is Viv.

Pat   Viv, sorry, let me tell you, if it's a pack of cards and one of them falls well you'd get a / domino.

Graham   Domino effect /

Pat   That means / the security.

Graham   National security, no you go on.

Viv   Oh wow yeh the / whole.

Leigh   Well yeh I mean it's all over the place now isn't it, a total fucking / shambles.

Short beat.

Eldon   Peace'll come one day.

Short beat.

Pat   You're dealing with two things all the time and if you're good you're ok but if you're not good you get whacked /

Viv   I can't imagine.

Beat.

But you're an officer?

Alice   But you're not in the action itself but /

Graham   Well. I am actually / sometimes.

Alice   Graham is in charge of the security on the ships /

Graham   I brought back a Vietnamese, a gook machete, it's in the back there. Helps /

Eldon   Oh yeh?

Graham   Helps with cutting away the shrubs.

Eldon   Handy this time of year mate.

Graham   No but we're fortunate to make good contributions.

Beat. She's put him in a hole.

Leigh   Oh this is good.

Eldon   Delicioso.

Pat   You should tell them.

We were involved in a rescue.

Graham   Oh well. /

Pat   It was a heroic moment and Graham saved several gooks.

Alice   Yes / which was.

Graham   They got caught, the fishermen I mean in the tropical / storm with a fairly high sea they were blown out into the South China Sea. Many of them were barely alive when we found them.

Pat   The bloody yoons were lucky.

Beat.

Leigh   That's terrible, please don't call them that.

Pat   They didn't shoot at you.

Alice   They are human beings and they weren't soldiers, right?

Pat   Let me tell you, you never know. They're all sorts out there! Rapists and murderers and all sorts!

Alice   Gosh Pat. I'm so / sorry Leigh.

Leigh   No no.

Graham   We have to get communism on the back foot.

Pat   It's a pack of cards.

Leigh   Yeh, I mean, well I have a different view about that of course but /

Graham   Right.

Eldon   Let's get that record on.

Viv   Hang on love, anyone want some more?

Eldon   Everyone should be happy!!

Alice   Sorry we shouldn't have gone into those subjects! Haha. Oh . . .

Beat.

Eldon   Like I said all you can ask of me is to go back to Cadiz, that's all I'll say to you.

Alice   Oh! I dream of going to Europe.

Graham   Do you want a beer?

Eldon   Always mate.

Graham *goes to get one.*

Eldon   I'm going to sing a song, liven things up!

Viv   Watch out /

Graham   Well I'm not sure /

Pat   Oh! A song.

Eldon   So this is the one I said, I said the dancer, yeh that you looked like, Alice!

Viv   Oh no!

Eldon   So yeh, here goes.

Eldon *begins to sing a song in Spanish.*

Eldon   Cheers mate.

Pat   Oh it's so jolly and exotic! I really do love it I have to say.

Leigh   You're actually pretty groovy.

Beat.

Alice   Oh wow.

Leigh   You're good.

Eldon *sings a few lines, stops and there's a lull.*

Viv   That isn't the song he was singing – she was dancing, Alice, we'll put it on and /

Eldon   We'll show you how she was / you're . . .

Viv   It was another song, he just can't sing it!! He can only sing that one /

Eldon   Oh but the dancers! You should have seen them.

She puts the record on. Ad lib the fact that this is the song that they wanted to have on.

Pat   Oh it's so jolly and exotic, it's so jolly and exotic.

Alice   Yes.

Music starts again from the record.

Leigh *starts dancing,* **Alice** *joins in, moment of happiness.*

Viv *turns the record up.*

Leigh   Ha ha.

As the dancing goes on, it isn't as though **Alice** *and* **Leigh** *are dancing together exactly, but rather that* **Alice** *is getting more and more carried away in her dancing.*

Eldon   You're just like the dancers, I told you she's just like the dancers. Olé chica!

As **Alice** *begins to dance, there should be a sense of people watching her, unsure what to do. It is the dramatic climax of the scene, and* **Leigh** *gets involved in the situation more than the others.*

As the music rises and rises, **Alice** *falls over and knocks over the chairs,* **Leigh** *rushes to pick her up.*

Graham   That's fine, you have her mate.

Leigh   .

Alice   What are you /

Graham   No no you have her.

Pat   It's ok he's /

Alice   Graham I'm just / dancing.

Leigh   Yes, there is nothing going on here mate.

Graham   Yeh yeh, no it's alright. You better shut up.

Alice   Graham.

Graham   It's alright.

Leigh   Sorry, look, it's my fault. I'll go.

He sits back down.

Eldon   Oh well that /

Viv   Yes.

Eldon   That was a terrific evening, simply . . .

Alice   You don't need /

Graham   I think well /

Pat   We need to be at base tomorrow so . . .

Alice   .

Pat   Yeh thanks.

Pat/Viv   Do you /

Viv   Yeh?

Alice   No it's nearly all done.

They are left alone.

Alice   Do you want anything /

Graham   You were out of control.

Alice   I'm sorry / I

I thought you liked it when I danced . . . you / said I was a good dancer.

She tries to be forgiven for it. **Graham** *is appalled and attracted. And she's a bit drunk now.*

Graham   You're not a schoolgirl anymore.

You're drunk.

Alice   I'm not.

Alice *laughs a bit like her mother.*

Graham   I never know . . . what humour you're going to be Alice, one minute you're happy and the next you're well, perturbed. I never know what you want.

She is cleaning everything else up.

Graham   So I've been thinking . . .

Alice   Yes . . .

Graham   I'm ready for children.

He looks at her.

We should do it now, tonight, as I'm off tomorrow.

Alice *goes back out towards the kitchen, anywhere, to get away.*

Alice   But I'm not ready /

It's just I want to try and / uni . . .

Graham   Alice you've failed uni, and that's that's ok!

You don't need to set the bar at an unrealistic height for yourself. You wear yourself out.

Alice   But /

Graham *begins to lose his temper.*

Graham   I will kiss you between the legs, if that's what you like. Loosen you up.

Alice   I /

Graham   Alice I want you. This evening before I go away.

Alice   I'm tired!

Graham   Come on Alice . . . I'll not be long,

Alice *decides to go with him. This could be done by smiles.*

Four

One month later.

The theatre main curtain closes and we are now in the main auditorium, and just before it closes **Joss** *(fifties) comes through the curtain.*

House lights are up. We are in a lecture theatre in a college of further education.

Joss   So you have a choice.

Passionately.

I think sitting here now, the question is, what vision of the world makes sense to you?

If you choose this course, that is what we will investigate.

I truly love poetry. It means everything to me.

The world is never the same once a good poem has been added to it.

He laughs.

Really what it comes down to is WE HAVE TO COMMUNICATE.

To communicate, truthfully, sincerely, is a revolutionary act. And that's where the politics in 'poetry and politics' is in this course title.

Do this, buy that, marry them, eat it, drink up, follow him, be her. Meanwhile poetry is there, an ALTERNATIVE, in the folds of the world. It is an act of resistance, defiance. A secret revolution that begins in the heart. You have a choice.

To break free from the chains of the world, from sleep from death . . . the readiness is all, says Hamlet. The readiness is all.

> Ay, in the very temple of Delight
> Veil'd Melancholy has her sovran shrine,
> Though seen of none save him whose strenuous tongue
> Can burst Joy's grape against his palate fine;
> His soul shalt taste the sadness of her might,
> And be among her cloudy trophies hung.

Poetry makes you an active citizen, since you are IN THE World, you can feel it you can sense it. It matters. And injustice matters.

Any questions?

Short pause.

Someone in the audience puts their hand up.

Maddie   Hi there, Maddie Thompson, first-time student.

So what you said was very nice, and I understood most of it.

I was wondering sort of what should we expect from the course. Are there a lots of assignments?

Joss   Well, let me turn that around to you. What do you expect?

Maddie   Well, I'm an avid reader. I read *Australian Women's Weekly*, weekly.

Joss   Good, good.

Mad   So I'm hoping to do more reading, and well, get better at it.

Joss   Good, good.

Joy   Hello yes, are we on a first name basis here Mr Owens?

Joss   You can call me Joss, yes.

Joy   Joss. Joy. Ha! Well some of us attended a course you did here last term, Voices from the Bush – Australian Female Pastoral Poetry, and well, all I can say is it got me really really really fired up.

I think a few of us were on that course weren't we?

Looks around at another member the audience. Ad lib is good here.

Well what I really wanted to ask is if, well, if we can offer some of our own poetry too / because I have some . . .

Joss   I think well, I would certainly encourage you to write your own poems I think so, yes.

But this course will be focused mainly on the analysis and discussion of poetry and its application to the world.

Well if there are no further questions we will be seeing more of each other anon I daresay. Thank you.

A beat – the students exit. **Alice** *lingers.*

She walks up onto the stage, and then right off it again.

Joss   Yes? Can I help you?

Alice   No no.

Joss   What were you wanting to / say

Alice   No I, well.

Joss   Yes, hello.

Alice   Hello.

What you said was really important to hear, it made a deep impression on me.

Joss   I see /

Alice   Yes, it spoke to me very profoundly.

I'm incredibly keen on the ideas you spoke of the idea of rising up / revolution

Joss   Yes, really oh /

Alice   That the well what really matters is a kind of sincerity a directness . . . I don't know, I find DH Lawrence really, I mean.

Joss   No I love Lawrence, particularly.

A temple / was never perfectly.

Alice   A temple till it was ruined and mixed up

With the winds and the sky!

Joss   And the / herbs.

Beat, silence, looks, attraction. They talk all at once together.

Alice   I'm no poet just an art teacher at secondary school so don't expect reams of lyrics from me.

Joss   Well you don't need to be anyone to be here. In my village, you know, everyone was in touch with the land.

Pause.

The animals and the humans. Alike.

He laughs, they laugh together, it is romantic.

So you could be a teacher or a chicken, it still rained all the time.

Alice   Well you'll see there are some parts of this country that could do with rain so your Welsh chickens might come in handy. And I'll certainly be doing your class.

He reads the name tag on her name.

Joss   Very good, Alice Betlam?

Alice   Betlam-Burns. Yes.

Awkward. But somehow love.

Joss   It was a pleasure, Ms / Mrs Betlam Burns Lawrence Keats. I have a class now but /

Joss *on his way out of the room.*

Alice   Sorry I don't usually go up to people but, well there was something in what you said.

He exits, she's alone. A beat of silence. She could look at the audience for a moment.

Five

Four months later.

Alice and Graham's house (as in 1.3)

*The curtains of the theatre open, revealing **Older Alice** sat on a single chair on the set. The set is somehow stripped back now, less real.*

*As **Alice** comes towards the chair, she gets up and leaves towards the audience. Stands halfway up the stalls.*

*Enter **Graham**. Beat.*

She goes to kiss him, to which he is reticent.

Graham   Sorry, I got held up didn't / someone

Alice   No.

I didn't know where you'd been.

It took me twenty minutes to get through the crowd and then there were the protestors /

Gosh it's such a thrill to have you home!

I was the last on the dock.

Are you ok?

Graham   I'm just assessing where the . . . tumbler that Uncle Rick gave me at the wedding is?

Alice   The tumbler, oh it's in the

In the cupboard there.

Yes.

Yes it's there. Graham . . .

Graham   No no, I just think you should leave it out

Because it seems natural that I would want a cocktail when I get home.

Alice   Sorry, yes I'll keep it in the /

Graham   .

Silence.

Alice   What's wrong?

Graham   Nothing.

Alice   You must be tired.

Graham   I'm not happy.

Alice   Right.

Oh. What do you mean?

Graham   I just, when I think to myself, I should be feeling a certain kind of way when we are together and when I'm home and yes, well, it isn't the way of things, really, Alice.

And our failure, to have a child, your resistance / to it.

Alice   My knee.

Graham   You are full of excuses Alice but they don't, well I I I I mean life is short, I'm nearly thirty, I've been on six ships in as many years and I'm sick of it. It's just that you're so staid Alice. What do you want? Have you asked yourself?

Alice   What do I want?

Faster.

Graham   We need to sell the house.

Alice   What?

Graham   Well I'll be needing the money for a matter, you see and . . .

Alice   What matter?

Graham   That's not your concern. /

Alice   Sorry? / Where'd we go?

Graham   You could go and live up in the Blue Mountains, look after my parents, there is a dependency there, a small hut where you could do your reading.

I would of course visit but I will be having to be away a lot, developing opportunities, and we should have a real talk Alice but you /

Alice   We are talking.

Graham   Well. It's clear that this isn't as it should be and the house was a big expense and I want to launch a business, get out of the Na/vy, and Pat.

Alice   No, I won't have that. I refuse. What about Pat?

Pause, she goes to the kitchen, comes back with a plate for herself.

Graham   What do you mean you refuse?

Alice   I refuse. I don't I won't do it. You can't just get what you want because you well you can't get what you want.

Graham   I . . .

Alice   I'm going to make some dinner.

Graham   ALICE! Wait there. I have this clearly ordered in my thoughts and you are messing / with it. I'm doing what's best for you.

Alice   I'm hungry stop talking.

Graham   You bitch! You always look down on me . . . you're so arrogant you think you're bette/r than me but you're not better.

Alice   Say what you want, it's all coming out now.

She laughs.

Graham   I'm sorry but we are going to need to sell the house.

Alice   I will sell the house and go back to study.

He laughs.

Graham   You can't, you're too stupid.

Alice   I will.

Graham   I bought / this house, it's mine.

My parents, my mum!! My mum!

Alice   Oh poor boy, poor boy . . . oh no . . .

Graham   MUM! Stop goddamn you, stop.

Alice *laughs.*

Beat. Eyes.

Graham *moves to push* **Alice***, to throw her off the balcony/cliff.*

Graham *needs to lay his hands on* **Alice** *and for a second we need to understand she is going to be pushed off the cliff.*

Alice   What are you doing?

Graham   .

Alice   What are you doing you're trying to push me off.

Graham   No.

No that wasn't / what I was doing.

Alice   I felt it. I felt it. I felt you think it.

Graham   No! no! no.

Alice   You wanted to kill me like . . . I saw it.

Graham   No you didn't, you're imagining things.

Alice   DON'T you tell me that.

Graham   Alice, love, I.

Alice   .

Graham   What are you thinking?

Where is the / I think I'm hungry.

Alice   You aren't.

Graham   Alice I didn't! You are / fucking lying. I didn't /

Alice   I want you to go.

Short silence, he almost begs.

Graham   No no Alice, please.

Alice   Leave.

Very fast.

Graham   It's my house, you can't bloody study NOW /

Alice   GO.

Graham   Look it was I'm pressured / I need a demanding job to keep my train of thought heading in the right direction.

Alice   Leave / Graham leave.

Beat. **Graham** *moves towards the audience. Panics.*

Graham   Forget everything I said. You won't manage without me.

Alice   Get OUT!

OUT!

Graham   I still love you.

I didn't mean it.

Alice   You /

Graham   No /

Alice   Go!

GO!

GO.

Then **Alice** *is alone on stage and the set begins to make a movement backwards and the stage shatters into pieces around her as the set deconstructs. The house separates into pieces, the walls are taken apart by the crew visibly.*

Act Two

One

Three years later. 1973

Alice, *assisted by* **Joss** *and* **Leigh**, *are moving her stuff into the storefront that* **Susie** *has. This should be a new space created out of the old one, a new start, a new page.*

Susie *is sitting on the sofa. Heavily pregnant.*

Leigh *enters carrying something.* **Alice** *too.*

Leigh   I'll just go and get . . .

Alice   Joss.

Joss   Fucking boxes.

Leigh   Yeh the door isn't that easy is it / I mean yeh

Joss   No but the /

Leigh   Yeh I'll go and get the

Susie   Alice this is so wondrous I can't believe / you're here

Joss   Where does this go fucksakes /

Alice   I'll do it with you.

She does.

Susie   We're going to do so many things together and when Eal is born /

And /

They embrace.

Alice   I brought everything! Is it too much?

Susie   No, I could never get round to getting anything for the place so it's great! Yeh! / I just have my bed and my camera.

Alice   I could put some in storage / or

Susie   No no I want it all here!

Stop IT!!!

Alice   I just took ALL of it. I wasn't letting him have any after /

Joss *comes back with books,* **Alice** *stops in her tracks.*

Leigh *with something else.*

Joss   I hate sweat.

Leigh   Go back to Scotland then mate.

Joss   Wales.

Susie   More books.

Joss   She has some reading / to catch up on.

Alice   I'm fine oi.

Alice *goes out with* **Joss** *again, leaving* **Leigh** *and* **Susie**.

Susie   Leigh darling!

Leigh   Susie darling.

They kiss on the lips theatrically.

Susie   Divine to see you!

Leigh   Is Eva here?

Susie   She's out back. Yeh stormy /

Laughs.

Alice *enters carrying a table, alone.*

Susie   Bob and Peg.

Where shall we put it?

Susie *moves the table around.*

Joss *goes to the loo.*

Joss   Let's go see what's wrong with your fucking tap.

He goes there.

Leigh *is in the corner, rolling a cigarette. Or similar.*

Susie   Let's be fuckin crazy.

She breaks the table angle, so the furniture in the space is somehow more eccentric.

Alice   Oh!!

Susie   Where d'you want it?

Alice   Oh.

She realises she doesn't know.

Susie   Alice just decide.

What do you want!

Alice   Oh fuck!

Susie   Have you asked yourself where you want it!!!!

Alice   AH!!!

Here.

Susie   Actually I think it's better over here.

She goes towards **Leigh** *to get a swig of the whiskey.*

Leigh   I'm so happy for you.

Alice   Sweet Leigh, you know if you'd not come to dinner, I think now, I'd be /

Leigh   Well yeh I mean that was a lucky / escape.

Leigh *notices* **Eva** *(fifties), who comes up behind* **Susie** *and holds her, they embrace.*

Eva   So this is Alice?

You're the soldier's wife . . .

Alice   Yes, well. I divorced the / you could say.

Eva   Good to stop fucking murderers right.

Short beat.

Susie   Eva. Alice.

Alice. Eva.

Alice   I've heard so much about you, it's just. Gosh it's /

Eva   Yes yes good to meet ya.

Alice   I've seen you on campus and obviously I loved your lectures, especially on Eliot and /

Eva   Yeh? Oh great . . . well I dig Eliot hard so.

Alice   Yes me too.

Susie

Alice   No of course. I've heard so much ABOUT YOU also from Joss . . . /

Eva   Yeh right is he here?

Alice   I was actually thinking of joining one of your poetry groups /

Susie   You'd have met but she was in England . . . with Germaine . . . yeh . . .

Eva   Who's got a drink /

Alice   Sorry / no I'll get you one I just

Eva   It's ok doll we serve ourselves here. No more serving for you.

Alice *in the middle, left hanging.*

Susie   Oh so your mattress, let's just put it here for now . . .

Eva is kind of using that room as a study for now . . . But she's going to the US soon and it'll be yours, bu/t

Alice   No yeh fine /

She pecks him on the cheek.

Joss   Finally, the arc is loaded, the sheep, the mule and the rat are all ensconced within the womb of the boat.

And SHE can set forth for her glorious voyage, her journey of the sea, wherein she flies /

Eva   Fuck me that's bad.

Joss   Eva.

Eva   Hi Joss.

Joss   Is there any of that wine /

Eva   So are you two entangled.

Joss   I DON'T SEE any rope.

Where is the twine?

He laughs nervously.

Eva   So you're fucking?

Beat.

So you're definitely fucking?

Is that new, it must be?

Alice   We've known each other a bit / but it's been a few / months yes.

Joss   Three years ago she came up to me like a gust and /

Eva   When he was teaching housewives.

Alice   Oh do have some?

She is talking to **Leigh** *in the kitchen.*

Leigh   Sorry. No thanks yeh. I've started early today!

Alice   It's all to be drunk!

Susie   Ok I'm hungry

Shall we all go to the Sussex /

Joss   Well there'll be a crowd down there /

Faster.

Eva   You've absorbed your conditioning quite well / if you think he's your ticket to liberation doll.

Susie   Stop it for a second.

Eva   He's an old flame of mine, barely a spark, a flicker of a fuck if you ask me, did he tell you that /

Alice   Yes. Of course.

Eva   Good, well / he's a lousy lay isn't he.

Alice   No he's a great fuck.

They all laugh. Short short beat.

Eva   Ah well.

Leigh   Yeh Joss has been woken / up by Alice.

Eva *glares at* **Leigh**, *he backs down.*

Susie   Where are your pictures, we could put them up /

Alice   Oh no I don't have them. I left them at my mum's.

For **Eva**'s *benefit, tough, clear, owning it.*

Alice   I don't talk to her so.

Eva   Cool no ye/h

Alice   She was so upset when I left him. She kept inviting me round and springing him on me /

Eva   Hard knock life.

Susie   Babe you should have seen her drawings

THE BIRD, was it a pelican? Some kind of wounded migrating bird . . . blood dropping / as it circled the sea

Eva   What the fuck.

Alice   I'm not an artist, but I'm / I did that when I was at school!

Susie   It was brilliant /

Alice, *from here and as much as possible in fact in this scene should speak fluidly and confidently.*

Alice (*to* **Eva**)   I write about art.

Eva   Have you published?

Joss   She is bloody brilliant.

Eva   So you haven't published, let's go to the fucking Sussex. Joss. / Come on Joss.

Susie   Oh, you?

Eva   Yeh look you just said you wanted to go /

Susie   No no yeh . . .

She holds her stomach.

Alice   Oh!

We'll just /

Joss   Yes, we'll finish up here and join you.

Leigh   Fine /

Eva   Come on. /

Susie   Bye . . . bye . . .

Fucking hell.

Eva *notices that* **Joss** *isn't coming with her.*

Alice *and* **Joss** *are left alone.*

Alice   Oh.

God.

Joss   I would be quite happy for you to eat me Alice, I mean you could eat me alive, and I wouldn't . . .

Alice   Me too.

Joss   No but I really mean that.

Alice   Joss.

Stand there. Let me see you.

She begins circling **Joss**.

Alice   There

Fuck

Joss   What are you doing?

Don't look at me like that

I feel naked

He begins to cry.

Do do do

With me . . .

I'm so totally yours

Alice   I want all of you, I want your . . .

Hands and your hair and your bones and your loins . . .

Joss   Oh yes, Alice, yes.

Alice   Oh Joss don't cry

I am painting you. In my mind.

You're my picture

She stands still and then she begins to shout.

Aghhhh!!!!!!!

Aghhh!!!!!!

Joss   Oh yes, Alice I fucking love you.

Alice   I want to turn myself inside out so you can see me. I already feel like my body is blown up.

Joss   Delightful.

Alice   I freeze until you touch me and I feel like I'm ill . . . I'm freezing around you but then I know you're going to touch me and I know /

They get close but do not touch.

There is a silence, a sense of time being frozen.

All enter from the pub with **Terry** (*thirties*).

Susie   We saw Terry Martins at the pub and told him to come over to meet you.

Oh this is Terry . . .

Alice   / Alice Burns

Leigh   Man I /

Terry   Martins, Terry . . .

Eva   Fine Arts Chair at Monash Uni.

Terry   Youngest ever Fine Arts Chair.

Alice   Yes I'm going I'm attending your / lecture on /

Terry   In Melbourne?

Laughs. He has his mouth full of food as he speaks.

That should be a laugh. My mother is coming to the lecture.

Leigh   / why?

Eva   Mothers and their sons.

Leigh   I wanted to say, I loved your book.

Terry *laughs a falsely modest laugh.*

Terry   Yeh, god yeh the / reception was humbling, especially in the US.

You got a drink there darl?

Susie   Of course!

Joss   I'll have another Scotch Alice.

Eva   Serve yourselves you limp dicks.

Joss   Eva wants /

Terry   To talk about pantyhose rather than / Vietnam right.

Eva   Go fuck yourselves.

Terry   No, women need protesting above dead soldiers Eva. Scotch darling?

Eva   You've murdered us for centuries /

Terry   See what I mean.

Joss   Come on /

He looks around, in the fridge, finds something.

Eva   Aren't they waiting for you down at the docks?

Joss   You are such a bludger. I've fucking founded the Worker Education Association. / You go down to the docks

He eats. And laughs at once.

Terry   Eva's got more important things to do, our cocks won't castrate themselves.

Looks at **Leigh** – *who walks off.*

Alice   Some women want to have their cock and eat it too. /

Eva   Right on.

Leigh   Yeh!

Flirting.

Eva   You're making me awfully sad here Joss.

Terry   What did you say you were working on?

Beat, silence, **Alice** *takes the stage.*

Terry   Yeh? No go on I'm interested to hear, Susie said you were doing an MA.

Joss   She is bloody brilliant / oh.

Alice   Well.

Pause, she's on the spot.

Eva   Go on, tell us. Dazzle us with the ideas of a reformed naval wife.

Susie   I'm getting bored of your cruelty.

Leigh   Yeah go on Alice.

Susie   It sounded brilliant.

Beat.

Alice   I'm trying to write my MA on Watteau and solitude . . . but I have a book idea.

Terry *makes a sound that is mocking.*

Eva   That little ejaculation from Terry there is because he has written about Watteau, what you gotta s/ay

Terry   I don't think there's much more to be said.

Leigh   Well the thing about Terry is that he makes big ideas like, s/o immediate.

Alice   Well yes, my interpretation is a lot more personal, I mean . . .

Eva   I'm listening.

Ad lib interruptions and echoes.

Alice   Well my idea is basically that I want to write a book linking paintings to life.

So I'll write about several paintings in individual chapters and each painting will have unlocked a learning in my life.

Eva   Interesting, interesting, which painting?

Alice   Well for instance / Pierrot.

Terry   Gilles? In the original French.

Alice   That painting has taught me about choice. Choice in my life.

Terry   Oh the personal approach can get a bit teary.

Leigh *and* **Terry** *laugh.*

Beat.

Alice   Terry, my book is probably entirely in opposition to you!

Laughs!

Eva   Fucking thank god.

Terry   Oh that's a turn on darl.

Alice   I know you speak of its political power.

Terry   Well it is on the eve of the revolution and I'm a Marxist /

Susie   What's the painting of?

Alice   It's this picture of a clown, a figure from the commedia, who is with his group of players of entertainers in the forest, but he is stepping out of the frame, and the others are behind him, really small . . .

She sort of describes the picture physically so that we can imagine it.

And he is stepping out, life size, it's in the Louvrey isn't it Terry?

Terry   Musée du Louvre.

Eva   Yes?

Alice   Yes so, Terry, Pierrot, he's used to being a puppet. Well, now, he's stepping out of the painting looking at us, with his quizzical face asking: what should I do? What should I do?

Leigh   Yeh trippy.

Terry   You must be careful of narcissistic sentimentality, it can be reductive, that breaking of the frame you refer to I read as a symbol of the proletariat upheaval.

What's your fucking concept?

Alice   Well my fucking concept is that it's a more personal vision /

Terry   I offer a reading, you're just saying how you feel /

Eva   Shut the fuck up Terry.

Alice   What's wrong with that? I'm trying to write about art and how it can teach us to live, to tell the story of our lives/ my dad was a painter and so I was brought up in this way of looking at things

Terry   Well that's hardly a reason is it, Dad?

Alice   Sorry but the personal is political.

Susie   YEH.

Leigh   I can say I've / felt that in my life I mean.

Leigh *is cut off before he gets a chance to speak.*

Eva   Right on.

Terry   Depends on the person.

Alice   I want to write a book that people will actually want to read.

Eva   She's cool, you are one tough lady.

Joss   Well Alice I didn't see that coming.

Eva   Course you / didn't.

Terry *looks at the floor.*

Terry   Well if you're simple. And lacking any kind of critical framework at all / I'm sure they will read it.

Susie   Alice has got some interest from publishers.

Joss   She has a publisher interested.

Terry   Wow. Really? For that idea . . .

Eva   Cool it Terry.

Terry   No. It's nice to be able to have a conversation about ideas with someone so pretty . . .

Susie   I'm sorry I'm going to eat myself, let's go back down to the pub before the kitchen closes.

Joss   Come come.

Eva   Righ/t

Tiny beat where we see that **Leigh** *is somehow less keen.*

Leigh   I think I'll head.

Alice   Leigh?

Susie   I NEED to feed the beast.

Terry   I was just getting comfortable for this, why don't you pop your little tushie down here.

Susie   No I'm, well I'm just going to eat but.

Terry   Some hospitality.

Alice   I'll be right there, you go and

Terry   Well very impressive, I'll see you in Melbourne, you know when you're there, I could take you to see some artists' studios. Fred Mallensothman for example. Would you be up for that?

Susie *overhears this and is a bit jealous.*

Alice   Oh.

Terry   Yeh you know him of course.

Alice   I mean he's a huge deal.

Terry He's an old mate.

Well then I'll see you in Melbourne, we can go and meet Fred and we'll have a great time.

Ad lib exits and so on. **Alice** *and* **Joss** *left alone.* **Leigh** *lingers.*

Alice Ha! Well . . . I guess I'll go along!

Joss You were tremendous.

Alice He's such a big deal /

Joss So, listen, Alice. I told Eva I'd go back with her tonight . . .

Alice Eva?

Joss Yes.

Alice   .

Pause.

Joss Don't be a spoil, it's just a fuck. I've got to fuck who I've got to fuck, I'm like that.

Laughs.

Alice Did, what /

Joss Don't be so god damn / conventional.

Alice No I don't care.

Joss Don't be sad, you don't need to be sad, Alice, come on. You're very impressive.

Joss *is leaving, down the stage and through the audience.*

Alice I'm not sad, it's ok, sadness isn't sad, it's uncomfortable /

Joss Yes.

As **Joss** *leaves,* **Older Alice** *appears upstage in the distance. She begins to walk through the space, as if she's remembering something behind her,* **Freddy** *(sixties), a 'famous' artist, appears. As if from the next scene.*

Alice   But it will be creative. I can find it creative somehow.

Joss   Exactly.

Older Alice *wanders to the front of the curtains, as they close, the scene change begins upstage,* **Alice** *exits. We feel like she is about to speak, but she doesn't.*

Two

Freddy

A few weeks later.

Melbourne, the studio of a very much-celebrated artist.

Freddy, **Alice** *and* **Terry** *are standing facing out, looking at a painting, obviously a huge painting.*

Freddy   Yeeeeh.

Alice   It's incredible, the figures / seem to appear out of the darkness.

Freddy   Oh you see figures there / good, I see them falling into the void.

Terry   Well they are sort of shadows aren't they, not really figurative.

Alice   No it's just so f/ree.

Freddy   It's just the result of a feeling.

He looks at her.

You know just MOVING from the first marks to the full gesture . . . an act.

He looks at **Alice** *briefly as a way of strengthening his own thought.*

Alice   Yes. I don't know how anyone can ever feel so free to do that.

She laughs, nervous.

Freddy   Oh you just got to free yourself deary.

Alice   Yes!

Laughs, looks down.

Freddy   I just need to kind of feel I'm fucking the painting you know.

An act of orgasm that I need to perform on the canvas.

Do you know what I mean?

Terry   Yeh, absolutely.

Barely looking at her.

Freddy   Can I get you a drink young lady?

Alice   Oh thanks.

He goes upstage, pours a very large drink.

Freddy   I've always tried to enter into the land, I think the land is important for an Australian artist.

Alice   Yes. My father / was

Freddy   Something about it making us feel how far we are from each other. We are alone.

Alice   A painter.

Freddy   That's nice / you're

Alice   No I'm an art historian.

Terry *is near* **Alice**, *there is one gesture of affection that is unwarranted.*

Terry   I'll have some of this.

He gets a drink.

Alice   What time is it?

Freddy   Not yet midnight.

Alice   Oh well I'll have to head off soon.

Freddy   Yeh a couple of people keep calling young ladies who want to write about my work, maybe you know them?

Alice   What are their names /

Freddy   Shows my age. Being written about endlessly, fucking endlessly.

Laughs, they all laugh.

You been to Melbourne much before dear?

Alice   Only as a child, I came here with my mother, / on the steamer.

Terry   Can I get you a top-up?

Terry *goes up to* **Alice** *and touches her in a way she doesn't want to be touched. She flinches but no-one says anything.*

Alice   No thanks.

Short pause.

But I'm doing a lecture, actually. / In Sydney, not here.

Freddy   There's ice if you/

Terry   All good.

Alice   It's at the faculty, / to the undergraduate.

Freddy   I'll have to come and see you.

Short beat.

Alice   Where is the bathroom?

Terry   The bathroom, just there off the bedroom. You can't miss it. The bath. Takes up the whole room, you love your baths.

Freddy   Hahah.

Alice   Oh. Thanks.

Alice *exits.* **Terry** *turns to* **Freddy**.

Terry   I won't be too long there mate.

Freddy   You knock yourself out mate.

There is a beat. **Freddy** *smiles.*

Here there is an ellipsis, like the memory has broken down. There is an incredibly long pause, about 30 seconds. Then **Freddy** *goes to sit on the sofa.*

Alice *comes out of the bedroom. It's obvious that she is hurt. Her walk is affected by what has happened, she stumbles into the room, looks at* **Freddy**, *and sees that he's complicit.*

Alice   Do you have a phone?

Freddy   Yeh there's one over there.

Alice   Do you have a taxi number?

Freddy   Well not to hand. You'll have to dial directory enquiries.

Alice *walks over to the phone, she feels his eyes on her and tries to hide herself, exposed in the whole room.*

The curtains don't close, and instead, as loud music plays, a big scene change happens in sight, where the studio is dismantled, and **Susie***'s house is rebuilt around her. She gets herself onto the floor, into a foetal position, and* **Older Alice** *enters, as if through the door, carrying the suitcase, and places it down by her side. As she would have done.*

A large bath is wheeled in by **Eva** *and placed upstage.*

Three

The next morning, over the following weeks time is elastic. It is her birthday.

Joss *comes in, is near her, then so is* **Susie***. As* **Alice** *sees them.*

Older Alice *is in on the edge of the constellation.*

Joss   I came as soon as

Alice   Terry Martins . . .

Susie   What? No. / He didn't!

Joss *understands.* **Susie** *does too.*

Joss   I / fucking . . .

Alice   He pushed me against the bath / and did

Susie   What bath, he didn't . . . oh Alice!

Alice   And.

Said as if he is trying to convince himself of it.

Joss   Stop. I'll bash his fucking head in.

Leigh *moves into the image, he is there in the memory now as well – the sense of two scenes A and B happening simultaneously. Scene A is* **Susie/Alice/Joss**. *B will be* **Leigh/Alice**. *The* **Older Alice** *is there as well, she is staring right at* **Leigh**. *Two scenes happening at once.*

Alice *crawls towards her books to work on the bed.* **Joss** *is moving out of the energy of the frame of scene A.* **Susie** *is there too – it now should feel like this is a slightly different time zone – the time jump is thus created by the presence and physical rhythm of the actors.*

Susie   Don't work now darling

You should probably say something. To the fa/culty.

Joss   No don't talk to the faculty.

No no. Don't put yourself through that / Martins is . . .

Susie   Yeh but / what is she meant to do.

Joss   I'll fucking bash his face in but the faculty . . . / it'll just make a mess for her.

Alice   You're afraid of him.

Joss   I'm not fucking afraid of him . . . I just want you to do what you're doing continue what you're doing. Be happy . . .

Older Alice *looks at him like he's* **Eldon** *for a second.*

Alice   .

Leigh *is in another part of the space – what we understand by now is that he's not 'in' the scene.*

Alice *sees* **Leigh** *now, like a flicker, makes a movement towards him but only as if it's a mental movement of time and memory towards it.*

Younger Alice *is a few steps away and thus* **Older Alice** *can take her place.*

Younger Alice *is called back by* **Susie***'s voice, which is addressing her as if she hasn't moved and so we get a sense of displaced time and space. As she does this* **Older Alice** *takes her place near the bed – so that* **Susie** *and* **Joss** *keep talking to* **Older Alice**.

Susie   Yeh. No I mean everyone knows he's a / lech, what did he?

It's now as if another conversation is overlaid with it.

At the same time, in parallel, the **Alice/Leigh** *scene is beginning. So that* **Alice** *effectively is moving between memories.*

She goes up to her, takes her by the shoulders.

In conversation A:

Susie   Martins is the darling of the faculty.

Older Alice   No no don't say that.

Leigh   Rest a bit.

Joss*, in the other conversation, is now moving away, out of the frame.*

Alice   Nothing.

Leigh   Alice.

Alice   I . . . nothing.

I'm good.

A moment of mutual understanding. Perhaps a gesture of it.

I /

Susie *answers – from the other side of the stage.* **Joss** *is gone.*
Older Alice *has moved away so that this conversation feels like it's back to being with* **Younger Alice**.

Susie   Yeh. Alice, don't work today.

Alice   .

Alice *sees* **Older Alice**, *then turns away, avoiding her eyes. She's 'back' in a scene with* **Susie** *about 'not working today'.*

To be clear, by now, **Joss** *has exited.*

Alice   No no, I'm just, I just have to.

She hugs her.

(*Jumbled up.*) Just trying to get some thoughts together. It's just. I'm going to do. Write my book. I just need

Susie   Sure you do.

I'm surprised you went in an academic direction Alice.

Alice   What.

Susie   No nothing.

Alice   I'm writing my (*jumbled words*)

She looks at **Susie**, *who is halfway off now.* **Alice** *looks into the audience.*

Alice   I need to go to Europe!!!!!

Susie *re-enters.*

Alice   Get out of here.

Susie   You keep saying that's where all the good paintings are.

Peg *has come in and she sits herself on a chair.*

Susie *is gone, the way* **Joss** *went – the other side of the stage.*

Alice *and* **Peg** *are left alone.* **Older Alice** *looks at* **Peg** *and then turns away and leaves the stage.*

Alice   Mum how did you get in.

Peg   It was / the door was open dear, Graham asked for you/r

Alice   Yes.

Peg   I called the uni, you've not been going.

Alice   Yes, I've been.

Peg   I went to look for you there. They said you've not been since you went to Melbourne and that residential course the other week . . .

Alice   That's a lie.

Beat.

Peg   It's nice to see where you live dear /

Alice   .

Peg   You know you could /

Alice   I need the money to study Mum. I'm writing my book and Susie is putting me up . . . I'm happy Mum (*hides her face, almost crying*) at last. I'm doing / what I want.

Short silence.

Peg   Have you spoken to Graham, he's been in a bad way.

Alice   Why would I speak to him, why do you speak to him?

Peg   I don't.

He's not happy with Pat.

Short beat.

Alice   What. I don't care.

Peg, *now, as if to catch up what has just been said.*

Peg   Dad's good. He's not doing much. Sketching a bit.

There is a beat.

Happy birthday darling.

Alice *looks at her. It's her birthday today.*

Peg   I got you this.

She's holding a bag with a hat in it.

I made it myself, you know the Connells and I have been doing a millinery course, it's not much good but really they are quite lovely people. Really quite proper and lovely.

And I thought you'd maybe, you'd like it.

She goes forward towards Alice and gives her the hat.

Alice *throws it on the ground, stamps on it,* **Peg** *shrieks.*

Alice   I don't want to see you Mum.

When I FUCKING told you I didn't want to see you I meant it I meant I didn't want to fucking see you so fuck off now.

Peg   You said I could see you on special occasions and today's your birthday and /

Alice   You've poisoned me.

Peg   What, what do you mean?

Alice   Poisoned.

Peg   What I, I don't understand. You're my only child, my only child.

Beat.

Alice   All these sick ideas in my head, All these things you told me to do, I LISTENED TO YOU / god why did I Mum, why didn't I ignore you. You've cost me so much.

Peg   Oh no, no no.

Alice   We can never understand each other.

Peg   But you're my daughter /

Alice   No. I can't.

She really asks the question.

Peg   Darling I'm so sorry I'm so sorry what have I done that. I'm so sorry.

Alice   You had your wedding, you had me in your dress and married and now I'm trying to live MY LIFE.

Peg   You can't say that, I wanted you to be safe / and happy darling.

No one ever did that for me. I never got one iota of what you've had. I love you darling.

Peg *goes towards* **Alice** – *it feels like they could hug each other but instead she pushes her out violently, throws her against the door.*

Alice *looks at her.*

There is a pause, enter **Susie**.

Susie   Where did she go?

Alice   I don't want to see her. Did you let her in?

Susie   She's ok . . . 'Bob and Peg'.

She hums and then goes to put on music.

People are going to be there soon . . .

Alice   I don't need a party. I need to be alone and think about what I want to do.

Susie   Yes but it's your party Alice!

She won't accept that something is wrong.

What's this?

Alice   Oh no / it's from my mother.

Susie I'm going to leave . . .

Susie   People will be here soon!

A beat.

Come on Alice . . .

*Enter **Eva** and **Leigh** from different entrances.*

Eva   Happy birthday! Shots!

Alice   Hi Eva . . .

They hug.

Eva   Wouldn't miss it!

Susie   Oh whiskey!!

Eva   I got some really good stuff.

Leigh   Let's have a /

Eva *goes up to* **Alice**.

Beat, pause, an evaluation.

Eva   Hey what the fuck, what's going on?

Alice   Nothing.

Eva   So you had a run in, so what?

I know what happened to you.

Come on! Tough lady, you're doing some interesting stuff,
you should come meet Germaine when she's back. You're
not gonna let this /

Susie   Yeh.

Eva   So he sticks it in, what do we care? All it is is bad sex
babe, move on.

Laughs.

So he's a shit.

You're not going to let some guy and his fucking antics define you, I've had twelve abortions kiddo and and . . .

Alice   Yeh.

Eva   Fuck! I mean it's just you gotta mix it up, find a way.

You know I have a son, I never see him, but when I see him when they let me I look at him and I think – there is nothing you think isn't yours. Nothing. All men are murderers. They find a woman and slowly, they murder her. You know that now.

Susie   I don't /

Eva   Fuck him, you have a choice in this.

Shake it out.

Tough fucking lady. AGH!! / AGH!!!!!!!!!!!!!!

Alice   AGHHHH!!!!

Alice, **Eva** and **Susie** *all scream,* **Leigh** *laughs and joins in a little.* **Alice** *puts her hat on.*

Leigh   I love this song.

Terry *enters.*

Everyone welcoming **Leigh** *and* **Terry** *– hi! Terry! Etc etc.*

Terry *goes over to greet all of them.*

Susie   Terry.

Eva   Terry . . . what the fuck are you doing here? Fuck off.

Short beat.

Terry   I just thought I'd pop by . . .

Leigh   How are ya.

Terry   Good yeh / yeh

He goes up to **Alice**, *she turns white. Everyone notices now.*

She puts her head down, and the hat blocks him kissing her.

Terry   Haha haha, that's how you do it is it??

Somebody's not in a party mood.

Susie   Come on Alice you're ok yeh /

People know but don't do anything or acknowledge the reality of it.
Terry *here is playing 'it's all good isn't it'.*

Music just cuts out.

Terry   She's well she's sul/king, come on?

Eva   Shut the fuck up / Terry.

This is a moment. A short one when it is made real.

Leigh   Ok mate, yeh.

Terry   Yeh no, all / good.

Susie   Alice?

Alice   I'm not / I didn't say anything.

Leigh   Let's go yeh. Thanks Terry.

Alice   I'll be right there, I'm just. Can everyone please go.

Susie   What, Alice, no it's your / birthday.

Older Alice, *who has never left the stage but rather hovered in the darkness beyond the bath, comes in and speaks this line, she is positioned in a place not directly next to* **Alice** *–* **Terry** *answers* **Younger Alice** *with his eyes.*

Alice   Terry, stay here.

Susie   Come on Alice . . .

Eva   No we're all fucking off.

Now.

Everyone disperses and leaves through separate exits.

Terry *and* **Alice** *remain.* **Older Alice** *takes* **Younger Alice's** *place –* **Terry** *playing the scene as if to* **Younger Alice.** **Younger Alice** *goes to a space between audience and stage.*

Terry   I bought a bottle of wine . . . I don't know.

It's '67 Cab Sav.

Red.

Yeh, good wine.

Older Alice   .

There is a moment of silence between them.

Terry   Shall I open the / wine?

Older Alice   No.

Terry   Ok . . . yeh?

Darl . . .

Older Alice *is focused.*

Older Alice   What did you call me?

Terry   Darl.

Older Alice   That was what you said to me, Darl, when you.

Terry   Oh, no, yeh. . . but look you're not gonna make a big /

Older Alice   Thing of it /

Terry   No. I mean I think you're great you know, darl. You know?

He giggles. But he's nervous.

Yeh? I think you've got loads of really good ideas /

A beat. Danger.

Older Alice   I'd like us to have a bath.

She goes towards the bath. Stands.

Let's undress and have a bath.

You have a bath.

Terry   Oh yeah? I mean?

Ok.

Right well, as you say.

Haha.

He's a bit unsure now about what is being asked of him. He goes along with it, mainly out of a kind of denial.

Older Alice   Take your clothes off.

Terry   Yeah right.

Ok, then, yeh, a bath.

This is some kind of trick? Ha!

Older Alice   You did what you did to me. Now you take a bath.

Terry   Darl come on . . .

Older Alice's *look makes him not talk further.*

Older Alice   .

Terry *begins to undress. He is still thinking this is part of a kind of game. But beginning to doubt it more and more. As he undresses he feels that the atmosphere is not what he thinks it is.*

Terry   You know / well

Older Alice *after* **Terry** *begins to undress – has his shirt off – begins to undress, turning away from him. Changing the atmosphere in the process.*

They see each other in a state of undress. This is a moment of real worry for **Older Alice**. *She hesitates before keeping going.*

As she is nearing undress but he is naked she looks at him in the eyes only and says –

Older Alice   Get in.

He does. He sits in the bath looking down now, not yet broken but a little frightened, unsure.

She finishes her last items of clothing.

And she gets in. They are not touching at all.

Wash yourself.

Trying to cheer himself up. Save himself, keep it in a different place.

As he's washing himself, there is a beat of silence, then looking to change the atmosphere.

Terry   Is this how you do it is it?

He laughs nervously.

They stare at each other, locking eyes. Silence. He looks down.

He's about to say something. Sorry? He doesn't say anything. He is unable but she –

Older Alice   You can get out now.

They do. Him first, he does and is standing there.

She gets out after. There is a short moment where they are clearly separate and far from each other. She has done one thing and now, in the moment, makes a decision about the next step in the action. She moves towards the room.

Terry   .

Terry *is suddenly taken aback and has a thought to leave.*

Older Alice   Don't put your clothes on.

Come to the room.

Terry   Look, I think I'll just / go you know, yeh, not run over this again.

Older Alice   Come to the bloody room, we're not finished! Come on!

Terry   Ok! Yeh.

Beat. Now, **Terry** *shifts. He is trapped. He can't leave in case she really makes a 'scene', but then he sees that by staying he's going to have to face up to himself.*

Older Alice *goes to the bed and lies completely still on it.*

Older Alice   Lie down.

Terry   I . . . I /

Older Alice   .

Terry *does lie down. they both are completely immobile for a moment.*

Older Alice   You don't touch me.

Terry   Ok. I . . .

He goes to say sorry but doesn't. The moment is very live.

I'm / sor–

Older Alice   No.

Something in him breaks.

Older Alice   You don't just get what you want.

See, you don't get what you want.

Terry   .

Older Alice *goes towards where her clothes are and begins to get dressed, as* (**Younger**) **Alice** *comes and stands over the bed, as if taking her place in the scene. For a moment, they are both in the scene at the same time and they see each other.*

Terry *looks at* (**Younger**) **Alice** *as if to say 'I'm leaving'. He makes a movement. He is now not interacting with* **Older Alice**.

Terry   I /

Younger Alice *stops him. Could say 'wait'.*

Alice   .

Once **Older Alice** *is dressed, which happens onstage, she crosses a bit stage left.*

Terry *makes towards his clothes and gets dressed as fast as he can and leaves the stage –* **Older Alice** *watches him leave and continues to watch even after he is gone.*

Younger Alice *looks into the audience. The house lights come up.*

Then, a voice from the audience. It is **Leander**. **Leander** *in his current-day clothes (including cap) has unbeknownst to us been in the audience since an appropriate scene change.*

Leander   Mum?

Younger Alice *answers him first. But* **Older Alice** *turns visibly to see him/face the audience as* **Younger Alice** *is speaking, and will continue the dialogue thereafter.*

Younger Alice   Yes darling?

As **Older Alice** *turns herself towards him/the audience, slowly,* **Younger Alice** *moves off in a kind of circular way, off stage to the wings (i.e the two turns of the two Alices happen simultaneously).*

Leander   Would you like a glass of water?

Older Alice   No no, thank you.

Leander   I had no idea.

Older Alice   Yes, that was what I did.

Leander   So was that like when you left Australia.

Older Alice   I'm trying to keep the threads together, hang on . . .

But yes, I left after that.

Leander   What like you just left.

Older Alice   I walked out of Susie's days later.

(*Remembering.*) I went to Italy.

She smiles.

The back wall begins to move, pause.

I stayed in a little pensione in Florence. I had a room at the back onto the garden. I'd sit there and write to my dad, I tried to learn Italian.

I saw the paintings I'd seen only in books. I was lucky I got to do that in my life.

I was alone in Italy, and for days on end I didn't speak to anyone. I went on buses, tour groups in the hills with students, tourists, 'visit a vineyard' . . . see the churches, that kind of thing. I was drinking a lot of wine and, well, spending time alone. I met a few people, from all over the world.

Leander   You had a good time though? Right?

Older Alice   Yes. yes. I chose to go there, it was wonderful, then I chose to go Paris. On my own.

Leander   Yeh /

Did you see that picture, your favourite one?

Older Alice   Yes, I saw it.

Act Three

London 1982–1985 and the present (and Paris very briefly).

One

1982

Alice *is already present in the library. A librarian enters wheeling a trolley of books.* **Alice** *gets up and goes to him.*

Jacob *enters and goes up to the librarian. He is in his late fifties, scruffy, charming, trying to fit in. He goes to wait behind* **Alice**.

Alice   Hello there, could I just see if you've got my books?

Alice Burns.

Librarian   Yes.

Alice   *Social Work in Practice* and that one about Giotto.

Librarian   One second, they're here.

He goes off to get them.

Jacob   I have never seen someone read about social work and fourteenth-century art at the same time.

Alice   Art is, well . . . it's art isn't it.

Jacob   Of course.

Librarian *comes back.*

Librarian   Here you are.

Alice *goes to sit down but can hear.*

Jacob   Good afternoon governor.

Librarian   Yes.

Jacob   I would like to pick up some books.

He says his name quietly, as if he doesn't want to be heard. It's foreign.

Brukheim.

Shall I spell it?

He does.

Librarian   Yes.

Jacob   Thank you governor.

Librarian   Here they are.

He goes to the table and motions to the space next to **Alice**.

Alice *goes to sit in the chair next to* **Jacob**.

Jacob   Is this?

Alice   Yes.

Jacob   Thank you.

She looks at his books.

Alice   A history of socialist and utopian thought in Germany?

Jacob   Quite a short volume.

Alice   Hah.

And *The Confessions*.

Jacob   Rousseau, excellent.

Silence, she gets things out, eyes, movement.

Something happens in the space, some kind of commotion. Someone drops books – and then there is a moment of deep deep embarrassment from the feeling of the library.

Silence, actions, kindness.

Alice   I'm going to brave the British Museum canteen.

Jacob   Courage! I hope you're an archaeologist.

Alice   To dig into those cakes?

Jacob   Exactly so.

Alice   Would you care to join me?

Jacob   Oh no I couldn't possibly.

Alice *leaves and shortly after* **Jacob** *changes his mind.*

There is a silence in the library.

At this point, one of the people in the library is revealed to be **Older Alice**. *She just walks past as the curtains close.*

Two

1984

Two years later.

A house in London around a dinner table. **Alice** *and* **Susie** *are at the end of their meal.* **Jacob** *is doing all the serving.*

Older Alice *is in position in the kitchen sitting as a witness to the whole situation.*

Susie   Can I help you /

She gets up.

Jacob   No no /

Alice   It's ok, he likes doing that.

Susie   That was delicious.

Jacob   I can only do two dishes. Ratatouille and ratatouille with rice.

Susie   I'm not much of a cook.

Beat. There is a moment of awkwardness.

Jacob *is clearing the plates away.*

Susie   He's great.

Alice   Yes! We're good friends.

Susie   I'm so impressed you managed to change your life around, again!

Alice   I wanted to work in a more direct kind of way, so social work.

Enter **Jacob**.

Alice   Well I've kept a way of looking at things.

Jacob   Alice sees pictures everywhere.

Susie   I used to think I'd be a photographer but now all I do is take photos of my children.

Jacob, if you'd have known me in the Seventies, you'd never have thought I'd end up with three sons and a husband. I'm surrounded by stinking men.

Alice   Hah!

Susie   I find men fascinating. We didn't have any at school men at school at all!

Apart / from the baalll

Alice   Oh no.

Susie   That was where Alice met her husband . . . we were all dolled out dolls waiting for the ball on a shelf, we hadn't seen a man for months / just the nuns

Jacob   How Victorian.

Susie   They were awful the cadets they'd wait for the teachers to look away and feel / you up. Grab you everywhere.

Alice   Anyway we'd snuck in to the hall before the dance.

Susie   Graham snuck in too!

We hid!

Alice   Did we? I don't remember that.

Susie   There was this little stage and we jumped up on it and behind the curtains and we watched him come in the / little sneak.

Alice   Oh right.

Susie   We thought he'd gone but he must have heard us giggling and he jumped up on the stage and threw open the curtains! He chased us around the whole hall and grabbed our bottoms until the teachers came in.

She sort of mimes this.

Jacob   God!

Alice   He didn't! I don't remember him doing that. Gosh Susie, Rossy was there – he just called him back and / they left.

Susie   Alice you're deceiving yourself /

Alice   He was awful, he thought it was fun but when he saw our faces he was shy and afraid he'd done something wrong but he kept doing it.

Susie   And we all shrieked! He was a bit weird one wasn't he?

Alice   Well that we agree on. But I don't remember the chasing.

Susie   But then Alice was telling us he'd begun writing to her and she was in love, we were all so excited: what is it like to be in love. She even did designs, for a ring, a very intricate sketch.

Alice   Come on!

Jacob   Ha!

Alice   You're embarrassing me. That isn't what happened!

Susie   It bloody was Alice.

Jacob   It's ok, you can both remember it differently and it still be true.

Susie   Well you married him!

Alice   I did, god.

Short beat.

Susie   Where did you go to school Jacob?

Jacob   Not in a place like yours I think . . .

Susie   Where was it?

Short beat.

Jacob   Well right at the beginning when I was a little one it was in Vienna but after that, we moved around . . . before coming here after the war.

*Short beat, in which the contours of **Jacob**'s life appear for a brief moment. After a short pause, **Jacob** has a very small laugh, barely perceptible, that **Susie** doesn't know what to do with.*

Susie   No of course.

Right yeh.

Jacob   Ha!

Laughs.

Susie   Well our school was just crazy. Did you tell him about the Dawson thing?

Alice   Oh don't talk about that. / PLEASE Susie.

Susie   No but it was fascinating. Well there was this man called Dawson who had been locked up for a long time for raping and / murdering women, chopping up their bodies and scattering them in the forest.

Jacob   God . . .

Susie   Yeh, Australia, get as far away as you can /

Alice   Come on I've forgotten about all that / . . .

Susie   This Dawson character found his way to the school, he burst / into the chapel service raving. They had to call the police.

Alice   I never think about that / time.

Susie   I think about school all the time. I couldn't wait to leave but actually now.

Alice   Well, anyway, / who wants coffee.

Susie   Yeh he was pretty famous, right, it was exciting? All those bodies in the forest.

Susie *laughs.* **Jacob** *is upset.*

Jacob   I just don't really like talking about violence so much. I'm not, well I'm not so sure what purpose it serves.

He laughs to cover it up and make it ok.

Susie   Yeh! Sorry. /

Jacob   No it's ok, I'm fine really.

Susie   I always put my foot in it!

Alice   What are Pete and the boys up to?

Susie   They're at this *Return of the Jedi*.

But shit it will be over by now.

Alice   I'd love to see them.

Susie   We'd love to.

Thank you so much Jacob for a wonderful dinner!!!!

Alice/Jacob   You are so.

Welcome yes no.

Susie   See you so very soon. Who would have thought it'd be me visiting you in Europe?

Alice   Yes. Next week? Before you fly back.

Susie   Oh my god the flight . . . I didn't even tell you about it.

James and Eal were /

Jacob   It's a long way.

Alice *sees* **Susie** *out and then goes back to help* **Jacob** *clear.*

Alice   Thank you.

Jacob   Thank you my good friend.

Jacob   Dinner was a close call but it came out ok. I will wash up, then catch the last tube and leave you alone.

Alice   Ok! Sounds good.

She is on stage – the focus – and he is off stage.

He exits. Short silence.

Alice   I want your children.

This has to feel completely unexpected.

Jacob   What do you mean? Sorry.

What children?

Alice   Sorry that came out.

Are you keen on me?

Jacob   Alice we've never even held hands.

Alice   No but I want to.

Jacob   Some people have luck in life, some not. I have been happy but I can't say I've been lucky.

Alice   I want to be with you in a . . . romantic way /

Jacob   My luck is improving.

Alice   I see you Jacob.

I want you to see me, all of me.

You are kind. The world is full of hard surfaces, and you know that and I know that. I don't really know what I'm saying but you are what I want.

Jacob   I didn't see this coming Alice! I'm 55, do you mind?

Alice   I'm 42.

Jacob   You always said you didn't want children.

Alice   With you I imagine I can have children. With you, babies with you.

Jacob   I always felt my lot was to be on the sidelines of life Alice. It seems to me life is happening 'over there'. /

Alice   You can stop that now, you have a choice about what you do in this world.

Jacob   I've chosen to stay in the shadows, it's easier that way /

Alice   Well, one thing I know, and my life has gone around in circles. but it's, well, it's that sometimes you don't know what you want, and you spend long periods sitting there, not moving, treading water, maybe . . . what should I do? And then sometimes you know and then you do it and you have to have faith in it, that's what I know. I'm really not much / good.

Jacob   No no that's not true.

Alice   Well this is my choice, what is yours . . .

He chuckles.

Jacob   I'm sure I'm not the right person, something wrong with me.

Alice   What do you want.

What do you want.

Jacob   I'm nothing to write home about!

He laughs.

Alice You're wonderful. And it's what I want.

Jacob Are you sure?

Alice Yes.

I am so sure.

Jacob I have never felt so light Alice.

Alice Wow.

Jacob I am yours, whatever I am worth I am yours.

They clasp hands for a moment, laugh riotously. **Jacob** *disappears.*

Older Alice *who has been there throughout, laughs with* **Alice***, as crew come in with furniture, slowly building some small elements of a house around them.*

Three

1997

Alice *and* **Older Alice** *laugh together as the scene changes around them.*

Upstage, **Leander***, 12, begins to walk across.* **Robbie***, 11, throws a ball onto the stage from the audience.*

Leander Mum!

Robbie MUM!

Leander You're so fucking sad, I can't believe you're so sad.

Jacob Come on boys, come with me . . .

Robbie Can we go to Burger King?

Jacob Yes.

Alice No.

Jacob Come on, McDonald's or Burger King.

Robbie   Burger King /

Leander   McDonald's.

Robbie   The Whopper is a superior burger.

Jacob   Ok, let's go.

Alice   We can't just always feed them / burgers.

Jacob   I'm not. Alice. /

Leander   Alright grandpa.

Alice   Leander why are you so mean?

Leander   I'm fucking not.

Robbie   Why you so old Dad? I'm going to my room.

Jacob   I'm old but I love / you . . .

Alice   / Why do you have to be so cruel?

Leander   I'm not.

Jacob   Ok stop it now, let's go.

Leander   I can't be bothered. Bring us burgers Dad.

Walks out. **Jacob** *left for a second, he laughs. Looks at* **Alice**, *and there is a smile.*

Jacob   Lucky me!

They smile at each other.

They exit, **Alice** *is left alone for a moment. She then stands up, puts on a jacket, and we are in another scene.*

Four

2001

After the funeral of **Jacob**.

Robbie, **Leander** *enter the space, they have just come back from the funeral of* **Jacob**. **Leander** *is carrying a bag with a cylindrical object in it.*

Leander   Shall I leave this here yeh?

He puts a plastic bag on the table that obviously contains something, a box of some sort that has some kind of weight.

Alice   Ok.

Robbie   I don't think you should just, like leave it there. Mum?

Alice   Leander don't leave it there.

Leander   Where d'you want to fucking / leave it then?

Alice   Do you have to talk like that to me now, can you stop!

Leander   Sorry.

Robbie *goes to sit in the corner, silent. Silence.*

Older Alice   Ok, do you want to go and get some fish and chips? Boys?

Leander   What? How can you talk about fish and chips.

Robbie   Yeh I'm quite hungry actually.

Leander   How can you be hungry.

Robbie   What do you want us to do?

Leander   I don't know. Have some . . . solemnity.

Should be funny.

Robbie   I can eat and be solemn at the same time.

Leander   How can you talk about eating with Dad's ashes on the table? That's fucked, fact.

Alice   Darling don't say that.

Leander   What, it's true. Like the ashes are on the table.

Older Alice   Sweetheart look /

Leander   I'm not a child, I'm fucking fifteen Mum, and I don't need you to treat me like a baby. Like Dad died and you're /

Older Alice   I'm not but we have to be kind.

Leander   Fuck / this.

Leander *leaves the room.*

Alice   Leander.

Leander *goes off but not completely.*

Alice *drinks.*

Robbie *slightly and comically pushes the ashes aside to reach something to eat on the table.*

Robbie   I'm hungry.

All of what follows has to be played lightly, not aware of its sadness.

Alice   I'm just having a glass.

Leander *is afraid for a beat.*

Alice   I'm just having a glass.

Leander   What are you going to do, like, just drink now and cry and then drink and cry?

Alice   Don't be cruel.

Robbie   We should do something with the ashes.

He goes towards them.

Alice   I'm not, not yet darling.

Robbie *just eats.*

Alice   Not yet but soon we will. Of course yes.

Robbie   I think we should.

He could go and get the ashes.

Leander   We're not going to do it. We shouldn't throw the ashes away.

Alice   Come on darling /

Leander   No fuck that /

Alice   What?

Leander   I'm going.

Robbie   You're sick, we're not just going to live with his ashes in the house. There's something wrong with you / you psycho.

Leander   If you touch them. I'll fucking kill you too.

Robbie   If you're leaving then take them with you. (*Gives him the ashes.*)

Alice   NO! Stop it.

Leander   Fucksakes.

*He takes some out of the jar, he throws them all in the air, they land on **Older Alice**.*

Alice   Leander!

Robbie   Stop it!!!! Fuck!!! Stop it!!!

Alice   Don't worry, there's enough left.

Robbie *picks up the urn and takes it away.*

Robbie   I'll just put these somewhere safe.

Alice *has a little bit of a drink.*

Older Alice   What should we do?

Alice   What should we do?

Robbie   I don't know. Live I guess.

He begins to exit.

What about Leander?

Alice   Leave him, he'll come back when he comes back.

Older Alice *comes on and the two Alices have a moment at the table. The younger one has a drink, looks at the older one for a moment. They touch hands for the first and last time.*

Older Alice *turns to the audience.*

Epilogue

2019

Both Alices are still on stage.

Older Alice   I'm getting tired now . . . what else can I say?

Is this helping you? /

She thinks of going. She's had enough.

Leander, *now in his late thirties, enters.*

Leander   You know when I went to Australia last year, it rained the whole time, and in Kiama, the beaches were closed / because of sludge.

Older Alice   Why are you disturbing me with all this going to Australia, digging all this up giving me nightmares. I wake up confused, as if I'm in the house on the cliff /

Very matter of fact.

Leander   Sorry. I'm going soon anyway.

Older Alice   I know, it's getting dark.

Leander *is leaving.*

Older Alice   You know, the last time I was in Australia, years ago, I went down to the beach the night before we left. The ships were coming in, and the pelicans rushed out to meet them.

There was a little pelican who couldn't take off . . .

So mother came back.

There was nothing to feed the little one, so the mother just plucked at her own breast, some other pelicans flew down too, and did the same thing.

Beat.

The little one ate mum's flesh and quaked and quaked . . . and flew off.

Leander   Oh /

Older Alice   I walked on but the birds who had plucked their chests were overhead struggling, blood dropping on the sand around me, feathers and flesh, but they rose up somehow, soaring, their huge ancient beaks opening and closing, wailing off into the distance. I was left alone on the beach and the sea was loud. Hitting up against the rocks, it was getting dark by then.

And it struck me that it has always been like this.

Short beat, matter of fact, simple as possible.

Leander   Mum what do you mean /

Older Alice   It's ok, I'm all done with this.

Leander   I'd better . . .

She smiles.

Leander *leaves.* **Older Alice** *looks at* **Younger Alice** *and speaks to her and the audience with the last line.*

Older Alice   I'm not afraid you know.

Leander   Ok Mum, see you soon.

Leander *goes to leave. He leaves. As an echo.*

Older Alice   I feel like forgiveness is near.

The lights go out.

End of play.

Acknowledgements

There are many people that I wish to thank, but three stand out.

Faye Merralls, for making this play possible on every level, and for showing me life outside of it.

Rachel Cusk, for being an invaluable guide, advisor, inspiration and friend to both this play and to me.

And above all, to my mother, M, for your courage and love.